I0436938

Anagrams of Dialectic Antithesis

Ta Ne chi… Messia God's Altar in Fiat

by
Dr. A. Wayne Jones

authorHOUSE™

1663 LIBERTY DRIVE, SUITE 200
BLOOMINGTON, INDIANA 47403
(800) 839-8640
WWW.AUTHORHOUSE.COM

First published by AuthorHouse 11/16/05

ISBN: 1-4208-6170-0 (sc)

Library of Congress Control Number: 2005905096

Printed in the United States of America
Bloomington, Indiana

This book is printed on acid-free paper.

Dedication

One might say that the contrite outrage inured in this epic lamentation began in the Julian Age of 1441. It was under the aegis of that calendral reckoning that European "merchants" stole away a cadre of African men for the pleasure of one European prince. Because of the "lucrative" prospect of free black labor, in abundant supply, and available for the "taking" the Vicar of Christ declared our ancestors, the nursing mothers and fathers of civilizations, soulless brute beasts, post simians and sub humans scarcely above leaf eating tree swingers. Thus began the haunting furrow from which the 19th Century German anthropologists sumptuously tilled to harvest the academic theory of "benevolent abuse."

To my maternal great grandfather, Willis Davis (slave name) [and great great grandmother "Old Darkie"] who were kidnapped from (in all likelihood) *Kumasi, Ghana* and packed into the greasy fecal basted hold of an unnamed slave ship, I dedicate this piece. He was eight years of age when he was sold on the auction block in the year of 1847, somewhere in South Carolina. In later years he married my great grandmother, Henrietta, a full-blooded *Choctaw Native American* with whom he fathered 10 children. He died at the ripe old age of 107 November 20, 1946. To the rest of Grandpapa Willis' family (and mine) left in Africa - who escaped capture - and those who did not and are as yet unknown, I pay respect. And pray that this offering may contribute to completing our unfinished business with God.

Indeed, this dedication extends to all of the African Diaspora, as well as the colonized, and identity effaced children of Alkebu-lan unnumbered, unsung, and as yet unrequited in their (our) love of truth and freedom.

May our ancestors who prayed so diligently that we would both find and return to the way of truth (Maat), be vindicated in the awakening of this generation into the wakefulness from the nightmare of our God's chastisement. May we truly understand and rise from the bed of our dependency and, again build the house, community, and nation that too few of us realize we are.

To my parents, John Douglas and Bertha Earline Jones I make especial dedication, for it is their pouring out of life and truth into me that gave possibility to this writing. Because of you Daddy and Mother my heart and spirit has always been aflame for nothing less than the recovery of that to which we are destined - Fulfillment of the Life of the Almighty.

A. Wayne Jones, Ph.D.
2002 Anno Domini

Acknowledgement

The production of a work such as this is never accomplished without the aid and assistance of several profound minds. There are two that I would like to specifically mention here.

I am deeply indebted to the scholarship and encouragement of Dr. John Johnson, a man who is a pioneer and greatly gifted in God to elucidate the presence of Africans in the Bible, ancient, and modern history. I have learned more during single discussions with him than all the under- and graduate studies of the respective subjects. His reading of the manuscript and sincere criticism and encouragement further added to my resolve to pursue and complete its publication. He is the author of several internationally known titles such as the Black Biblical Heritage, God's Kinship with Dark Colors, Original Names of God and Jesus, etc.

In the course of yielding to the voice of God in bringing forth a new reflection of divine truth and insight into age-old maladies there are human voices which are the Muses of inspiration and destiny. That voice for me is none other than my beloved wife Patricia, my Lavender. She has ever been a constant voice of inspiration, love, and creativity. In addition to her relationship as Muse and Queen Wife, she with loving proficiency worked to transcribe my thoughts and words into a logical and concise format. Lavender, I love you . . . together we shall enter into union with Him Who is Truth.

There are many others that space would fail to accommodate, to all of them I say, "Thank you."

Author's Preface

Long have I wondered with profound perplexity why it was (is) that my people have suffered such unrelenting oppression and shame among all the peoples of the earth. Particularly, here in America the "rot" of slavery persists like a foul aggressive stench from which we have refused to wash ourselves.

The image of degradation not only haunts Africans in America, as well as around the world, but has abraded the psyche of most with a near-unclotted laceration of inferiority. I have often wondered if the condition of our people were not the "way of things." For a short while I abided the monstrous falsehood that Ham was cursed and therefore God was wroth with all things Black. It seemed, as was said, that we must accept our place in the "white man's and the White God's" world. That place of always being less-than.

I want to be extremely candid, dear reader, I am in no way (any more) resentful toward the Euro-American, neither contemporary, nor historic. Nor, do I harbor hatred toward the *Europeanized Christian Church (born ca. 312-457AD)*. I now realize that he was only a brittle alloyed instrument in the hand of the One Who is greater than all.

I have further come to understand that our condition is not the blame of the White Man or the American Government. Notwithstanding, the duplicity and dirty tricks imposed upon Africans with and without the aid of "so-called" Black leaders, deceivers, bleeders, breeders, and feeders. They are most to be blamed for the state that we find ourselves in at the cusp of the Third Millennium.

Candid study of African history beginning at the beginning, reveals profound evidence that what has happened to us was not, and could not have been, the work of mortal men; much less that of the recessive albinoid. Our current, but reversible state, is not the result of *a curse of Blackness*. It is rather the result of *our aversion to the Blackness* conferred upon us by God Almighty Himself, in the Person of the Pre-Incarnate Christ, the Father, and the Holy Spirit.

My dear African siblings please read this reflection in the spirit with which it is written. We stand upon the pivot singularity of the Day of our Visitation. It is time that we look again into the mirrored Face of God, as did Ethiopian Adam (Atum) upon his awaking into life. Look must we into the Face of God as we did so long ago with fullness of love, worship, adoration, understanding, and submission to His pleasure. Haply, that what He wrought in us may find expression in this nascent 21st Century generation.

This poetic philosophic lamentation intercession has been in the making for better than one half a century. It may be truly said that the words and urges herein have written me. And these cathartic, prophetic, apocalyptic *Anagrams* are but the gushing bleedings from the punctured arteries of my long assailed spirit. These

Anagrams are more than an uncovering of our self inflicted wound… they are an unshrouding of the way to our liberation and healing. ***May you be one of the few who will say yes to The Lord God (Jesus Christ) in this long awaited, long prayed for hour.***

A. Wayne Jones, Ph.D.
St. Louis, MO 2002

Introduction

This writing is called **Anagrams of Dialectic Antithesis** because of the manner in which it presents the historic and cosmic cycles of Africa's beginning glory, following decline, and certain restoration. The literary device used to accomplish this is the dialectic communicated through anagrams of the 13 key attributes conferred upon her by Jehovah. The description of Africa's present condition, degradation, and oppression is the *antithesis* of her ancient glory. As this writing progresses the eternal pleasure that God derives alone from Africa (and pan-Africans) is made apparent.

Through the use of this literary device our ancient ancestors' accountability for the present state of affairs is contrasted with this generation's accountability for ushering in the Restoration of Africa to God. Throughout the entirety of our history God's favor upon us has never been withdrawn.

This truth is evidenced in the title's anagram, *"Ta Ne chi... Messia God's Altar in Fiat."* Ta (land of) Ne (black, variant form of Neter - god) chi (life-force, spirit)... Messia (the Anointed One, Christ) God's (belonging to God) Altar (place of sacrifice and acceptance – where the power of flesh is slain and spirit is released) in Fiat (will, command, and sanction). *In other words Africa, also called Ta Neter (land of God), is the land of the Spirit of the Black God, and the land, as well as its people is Messiah God's altar upon which He has chosen to heal and redeem mankind – through sacrifice.*

The message of Anagrams of Dialectic Antithesis is uniquely structured to identify underlying ancient African modes of spoken and written thought forms. Among the most commonly used literary devices found in ancient Egypt (and continental Africa) were *puns*, *palindromes*, and *anagrams*. The very language of our Khemetic ancestors, the *Metu Neter,* lent itself to such significant variations of thought form and meaning. The Metu Neter, hieroglyphics according to the Greeks, itself means the *"words of (the) god(s)."*

Imagine, the very language of our ancestors was, by their own admission, the daily characteristic expression of principles that communicated the divine revelation of the Creator and fundamental laws of the universe. At the pivot of Deity and Cosmos is the African, microcosm of all that is. It was this that the ancients from earliest pre-Egyptian times expressed in the Metu Neter.

In fact, ancient Kush (Ethiopia), the land of Adam the first man (Genesis Chapter 2), used this language as its common medium of communication. It was in Egypt that it came to be used as the sacred language and repository of all science and theology.

Anagrams is written in a counter clockwise spiral presentation of 13 principal words. These words are the foundational characteristics of our ancient fathers as they were/are seen through the eyes of God. They are also the thesis (beginning) state of ancient Alkebu-lan, *the Mother of Mankind,* and mark the position in which we Africans began in the earth and Universe.

Those 13 words are used to express the progressive decline, fall, and ultimate restoration of Africans through use of dialectic presentation (thesis, antithesis, and synthesis). However, the words used to accentuate the aspects of Africa's historic and cosmic cycles are the key words' progressive anagrams.

The four sections of "Anagrams" following the opening reflection, The Verdict of Providence, The Reversal of Disfavor, Restoration of the Stewardship, and Union with Truth contain a total of 52 key words, the 13 thesis-words and 39 dialectic anagrams that express both decline and restoration. The following chart shows the relationship among the 13 key thesis-words and their 39 dialectic anagrams, as well as how they flow through the text. The matching fonts show the sequence of respective sections and keywords. The 52 anagrams are written in all capital letters in the text.

Antithesis (opposite)	Synthesis	Return to thesis	Thesis (original state)
		The Verdict of Providence	
1. *SLAVE*	VASSAL	SEAL	**SALVE**
2. *CURSE*	RUSE	SURE/CUE	**CURE**
3. *BLIGHT*	GLIB	GLINT	**LIGHT**
		The Reversal of Disfavor	
4. *NEED*	END	DIN	**EDEN**
5. *AFRAID*	DREAD	FICUS CARICA	**AFRICA**
		Restoration of the Stewardship	
6. *SLAY*	ASSAIL	ALL	**ALLY**
7. *SCOURGE*	MORGUE	GRUESOME	**URGE**
8. *EEK*	PEEK	KEEP	**CHEER**
9. *VIOLATE*	OVULATE	ET AL	**VALET**
10. *OPPRESSION*	SPORE	REST	**PROSPER**
11. *POVERTY*	ROT	PROMISE	**PROVENANCE**
12. *DESPAIR*	RAPE	AIDE	**PRAISED**
		Union with Truth	
13. *OCCULT*	*CULT*	*OCULAR*	*ORACLE*

How came the divinely enlightened ORACLE, singly PRAISED by Atum[1], Yahweh[2], and Elohim, appointed PROVENANCE of Earth and the Universe, deigned to PROSPER Creation and God... how came the VALET of the Infinite, who possessed the secret of eternal CHEER, to lose sacred URGE and become ALLY of the profane?

AFRICA, melanin face of God, primeval Pangaea[3], Center and Capital of the Universe and of Earth... forever EDEN (Alkebu-lan[4]), Garden of God and Temple of His Presence. Seminal LIGHT of Truth in created order, CURE for Set's[5] sedition... SALVE for all interstellar ills and the Solar quarantine. Explorer of worlds, planets, and moons... past and present Companion of Jehovah, Friend of Aten[6]... how came we to dust - salt unsavory, trampled under foot?

> *What heavy gauntlet, the **Verdict of Providence**, which subjected "ankh[7]"to wasting, buried "Duat[8]" beneath the dunes, and reduced "Per-aah[9]" to a SLAVE. Yoked about by chains and manacles, enslaved in mind, stultified in spirit, and tormented in body is the shadow of "Maat[10]" who once borne the burden of Wisdom... embodiment of "Sakhu[11]." Now dimly does the "Negus/Nigiste[12]" blink in a stupor induced by mummified brain and aphasic memory of the day that began with night.*
>
> *Like a creeping glacial avalanche, unnoticed, irrepressible did the CURSE ascend out of the very soil that was furrow to the holy. Once silo*

of Orion's arm, chosen spiral of Apis[13] (Pesach) - the Taurean Constellation - now concierge to desert, dust, and drought… host to thistles and thorns. Though the placenta of opulence and wealth, no respite lounges here. Concubine of rape, object of contempt - others now gorge upon the succulent delicacies fresh gouged from our quivering womb. Oh, with what coveted anguish do we now abort our precious fruit with blood-drenched grasping hands that ply, in self - effacing determination, visceral-lacerating forceps. Umbra in situ, barren in utero, the depth of our judgement extrudes in fecund atrophy - grated fractured life.

What was once the nurturer of billions has now become the BLIGHT. Specter of starvation, offence to mankind, putrid, pathetic, vile, and repulsive off-cast. How came such contemptuous despite? Among all the nations and civilizations of man, none have been so abased, none are so perniciously pulverized. Like diamonds crushed under brutal pestle of the affronted Apothecary, our supra human insult of the Divine bound us to the cavity of His unyielding mortar… and our resin flows un-therapeutic. Once Therapist to all living, now languid are we as one feted for the rapist. What pernicious, persistent, permeating blight… spit out, spewed out, extruded out by "Ptah[14]" and desiccated, decimated, di-urined of God.

Plunged into NEED unanswerable by any but the Father, proud Africa and her mighty pharaohs were disfellowshipped - and all Eden with them. Clinging like a clammy leech-like membrane, the film and dura of vital sufficiency smothers and torments with an elusive yet pervasive itching near to madness. Like the seven lean kine dreamed by Pharaoh Thutmosis III[15], no feast of gorging upon kines of fatness may undo, nor have undone "this sanctioned pernicious anemia." We cannot thrive beyond Jehovah's invocation of insufficiency. Having been given all, our abundance incapacitates us, our excess exposes us and we lack the strength to bring hand to mouth. It was Atum (Adam) who initiated the nakedness; it was "Peribsen[16]" who charted the course to this poverty. By venerating the Cherub who had been denounced, degraded, and defrocked forevermore, God's ire was provoked beyond his patience.

Upon the enthronement of Lucifer-Set in the hearts of holy "Negus/Nigiste" certain destitution did follow and was sealed by Deluge. Pivotal in irony and pitiful in honor - the day arose, rather the night descended that would wrench the scepter of Enlightened Stewardship from the hand of Nubia/Kemet. Transferred it was to be, and to be unknown until another evening should arise.

Proud in our unchallenged and unequaled favor did our royal ebon ancestors disdain the Divine Invective.

Sullen, yet hopeful were the mighty Adami in the Promise declared between the fork of Rivers Pishon[17] and Gihon, the White and Blue Niles. Inscribed in the Metu Neter[18] was the certain appearance of Messiah, who would certainly slay the Serpent - for all time - and gather up the offspring of Atum into the receded Celestial City.

The impotence of three near-Messiahs'[19] anti-climactic cadence forged a fear and extruded a decadence that reverberatingly echoed Adam's whimpering conscience, "I was AFRAID." When suddenly his light went out, like the instant draping of night's dark shroud over the bare landscape fast following Sol's abrupt plummet beneath the parallax horizon, the shadow of Holy Disapproval emerged beneath Adam's feet - spilling his sooted silhouette upon the cursed sin-blotched ground. In like sullen umbrage, the Garden, expansive Eden, Mother Africa, indeed became the Darkened Continent. Though elegantly resplendent with life and lordship, she was now infested with the pandemic pathology, first spawned in Heaven.

It was this pandemic, this insidious viral "invitee" that would SLAY the earth. Even as Atum stood, half-clad, full quaking astride his stark summoned sinister shadow; half-contemptuous, half-remorseful, full cleaving to his startled wife; Paradise about him pouted and jeered. In Mother Eve's tear glazed eyes, the reflected degeneration of perfection cast a grim reverie of images upon sclera, iris, and pupil. In that moment, the very air became a SCOURGE, abrasive breezes, now such biting reminder of how forbidden succulence spoils to become the acrid, then aloetic bitterness more caustic than quinine.

The brooding Garden, now withered figs, a serpent bitten ficus, is vengeful against Man who, though forbidden, greedily felled the mighty and tender tendrils that once flourished in his light, and gorged on beckoning illicit delight. With wilted rancor the wilderness garden, in defiant inverse travail, sprouted *flesh-eating-Fruit* in stinging soulless mimicry of rebellious *fruit-eating-Flesh*.

Ousted from the face of Ta-Neter's[20] skull Adam would be constrained, now, to EEK out a living from an atrophying resentful earth. There thorns and thistles would taunt the abdicated Dominion he did VIOLATE, never to be known again until the end of the Great Week.

Laboring under heavy sorrow and sweltering exasperation, Adam, with Eve, awaited the Seed who would alleviate the OPPRESSION. Lucifer-Set, having now gained the twin delight of serpent's palate, ground the once illuminated Adami[21] into futile dark spiritual POVERTY. Working his craft, so successfully self-destructive, the sooted son of the morning, the once-bright light bearer, blinded the mind of Earth's mightiest generation with dimmed luminescence, itself damned to extinction.

When once "the anointed Cherub that covereth[22]" made his fivefold assertion, first pentagram of willfulness, in self-condemning iambic pentameter, he said:

i   I will ascend into the heaven high[23]
ii   I will exalt my throne above the stars
iii I will sit within the sides of the north
iv   I will ascend above the heights of clouds
v   I will be like the most High God

In silent unstirred patience did the Father know and consider all his thoughts. Watching from the unscaled heights that adorn the zenith of His Emerald Orbed Throne[24], the Father saw through the designs of the Infarcted Confidante as clearly as He peers through the transparency of the Sapphire Sea of Glass[25]. With seasoned longsuffering, unbesmirched, God answered in fiat, even as Lucifer, Messiah of angels, conspired in intent. What Yahweh Elohim, with perfect compassionate judgement, willed in thought, word, and melody, concerning his spirit-crafted son, His Throne echoed in lightnings, thunderings, and voices.

The utterings of the Seven Thunders were a warning, issued once, to the Reflection who would be the Light. When resolutely he heard it, he hardened his ways, his heart turned, and his resentment against Omnipotence gave birth to iniquity... gangrene of will, which hath no cure.

The Seven Thunders pronounced the judgement irreversible, irresistible, and irrevocable - stop now ere you be no more! Alas, proud Lucifer plunged ahead. In self-consumed ambition and drunken euphoric giftings he deluded himself with the Ultimate Blasphemy -- that the Father has been unfair.

Coveting what he could not hope to hold. Lusting for that which was impossible to contain, craving for the

Thought he could not fathom, and aspiring to the Omniscience supernal to his Universe… he seduced worlds, planets, moons, and perverted climes beyond the reach of parsecs.

The Seven Thunders echoed with deafening trochaic finality:

i   I will cast thee as profane out of the mountain of God[26]
ii I will destroy thee, O covering cherub, from the midst of the stones of fire
iii I will cast thee to the ground
iv I will lay thee before kings
v   I will bring thee to ashes

And with each Galactic Year[27] since, the luminescence of the light bearer cast a lengthening umbrage, one only the Tribunal knew. Eons and ages do testify to the far-flung reach of the sullen cherub's craft. Doth not Cydonia[28], in tearful remorseful exile, countenance that certain resolute denouement? Cosmic trodden, ashen with blood resin residue, the gaping sentinel of the once proud Aries is war proud no more.

Misshapen and deformed are all things that the Cherub has fashioned, no exceptions are the once glorious Demos and Phobos[29] - twin diminished fragments of his seminal hope to a Glory he could never attain. The wrecking of proud Lucifer's once uncontested cosmic domain is both testimony and indictment of the DESPAIR he brought to angels and menoi[30], and imposed on replenished man.

Blasted by Leviathan's[31] breath, scorched and singed upon rebellion's forge, Adam and Eve after suffering presumptive hope, anguished double loss in corruption and murder, then failed expectation in a last anticipated promise - they slipped beneath the shadow cast by the declining day. Three failed messiahs. Three seeds that bore no fruit of deliverance.

Out of the seed of the last failed promise arose the weed of the Garden - the enosh. Man at his most corrupt state, incurably wicked, habitually sinful without remedy. Upon his generation Yahweh grieved the making of man, pronounced a judgement for which none could offer sacrifice, nor atone.

The Serpent's corruption now complete, the thing God wrought slithered from holiness of worshipful communion into the abyss of self-veneration and the OCCULT. What was revealed of the secrets of Creation to the Vice-Regent of Earth and Cosmos, was perverted and profaned by transmuting it to an instrument for self-glorification. So was derived the alchemy of the Wisdom of Djehuti[32], the gnostic hermetic principles.

This bold affront to God was celebrated by the emigration from Ta-Neter[33] (the Land of God) to Ta-Meri[34] (the Beautiful Land). Man left the Holy in lust for veneration of the Adept[35].

On the plain of Giza stands Seshep ankh Atum[36], the Living Image of Atum (Adam). In solemn, yet sad, and resolute reflection does the Sphinx mirror the unspoken resignation of Adam. Only in his crestfallen son, Cain, do we hear the tortured musings of Adam, which was daily on his lips, though un-removed in his day, *"my punishment is greater than I can bear."*

Many have speculated the interrogative that fixes such grave resolve upon the countenance of Father Seshep ankh Atum. Much of it has been foolishness and flight of madness. Yet, upon that unfurrowed though un-joyous brow of our granite sentinel at Giza[37] a hint, just a hint, a deafening silent thundering thought can be heard echoing from that decisive moment of the first autumnal equinox.

> One heartbeat after the "press" of that
> smooth ficus pome dripped from the
> corner of his quivering lips, and his eyes
> were opened - with fear and trembling
> came also this desperate pleading,
> "when shall come *The Reversal of
> Disfavor?*[38]"

Before mighty and proud Africa would be restored, ere
the primal parents of humankind should find restitution
for the serpent's bite, she would stride deeper into
self-made salvation and venerate the CULT of self-
worship. Although Atum yielded to the dust during
the days of Enosh's abomination, he lingered to hear
the pronouncement of Enoch, the immortalized Ha-
Panach of the Metu-Neter scrolls. Enoch, Ha-Panach
declared that the day would come when Jehovah would
return and restore what was lost to them, coming with
ten thousand times ten thousands of his angels and the
saints enregaled in white. From that day Adam, Atum,
looked to the east for the arising of the King of Kings,
Regulus, Leo, Atum after whom Adam himself had
been named. It was this hope that was fixed in stone,
the choicest granite there on Giza's plain.

In hope, solemn resolute hope, does Seshep ankh Atum, now
immortalized in stone, await that day spoken of by Enoch.
As a stark unflinching sentinel, witness and reminder to
this 21st Century brood, so too did he watch in splendor
- and warning - over those in ages gone by from before
the Fourth Dynasty, through the Deluge, and all the sand
blasted kingdoms since. With one muted voice he declared,
**"for the RAPE of truth certain judgement will fall. In His
appointed time the Living Christ will remove the ROT
that has festered in our bosom, He will give the increase**

to the SPORE of Righteousness yet hidden within the folds of our sooted Edenic vestments."

With daring monstrous arrogance have we, the pride of Alkebu-lan, contrived, fathered, and yes authored every abomination of worship and every prostitution of truth that now plague and infest the hearts of the children of the earth. Centuries afterward, the Apostle Paul speaking by revelation spoke most truly of our pristine primeval fathers. They walked the earth in the living shadow and furls of the Almighty's tunic. They saw His light, heard His voice, stood in His Presence as a man stands in the company of a contemporary and knew Him with an intimacy only dimly approached by the redeemed of this epoch. Yet, they found Him but too common to hold precious and casually trivialized the Uncreated Godhead. Paul says of our venerated African ancestors, how truly, and how well,

> *"Because that, when they knew God, they glorified him not as God, neither were thankful; but became vain in their imaginations, and their foolish heart was darkened. Professing themselves to be wise, they became fools, and changed the glory of the uncorruptible God into an image made like unto man and to birds, and four footed beasts, and creeping things. Wherefore God gave them up to uncleanness through the lusts of their own hearts, to dishonor their own bodies between themselves: Who changed the truth of God into a lie, and worshipped the creature more than the Creator, who is blessed for ever. Amen.*
>
> *For this cause God gave them up unto vile affections: for even their women did change the*

natural use into that which is against nature:
and likewise also the men, leaving the natural
use of the woman, burned in their lust toward
one another; men with men working that which
is unseemly, and receiving in themselves that
recompense of their error which was meet.

And even as they did not like to retain God
in their knowledge, God gave them over to a
reprobate mind, to do those things which are
not convenient..."

Burrowing ever deeper into darkness and soaring higher into Judgement-appointed pride our fathers, our African fathers, lineage of Adam, builder of worlds and Steward of the Revelation of Truth could only OVULATE chimeras progressively grotesque and insulting to the Divine. While there remained among us the archives of revelation, with cold unrepentant disregard of Jehovah's truth did we civilize and forge the advance of Man.

As long as Jehovah countenanced patience toward our corrupted Stewardship, we - proud Africa - did PEEK into the secrets of the Universe and the realm of the Spirit. Traversing all disciplines of knowledge and meaning of life we remained among ourselves as gods among all flesh upon the earth. Now, cryptically extant in the Duat, Ma'at, and Sakhu, all things revealed unto the ancient exalted family contains the secrets of science, philosophy, and theology after which scholars, thinkers, and mystics seek.

Such knowledge divorced from the love of Him Who is Truth drove mighty Kemet into the MORGUE. For many centuries has this Steward People lay as a dead entity…insensitive to the purpose and call made eons ago. As one, of necessity, who finally succumbs to a virulent disease, Africa, Kemet was felled by self-infection. In the morgue of Jehovah have we lain, to be ASSAILED by His judgement. Like a dead man having no power to resist or even turn from the certain falling blow of chastisement, we, once-mighty Kemet, remain a perplexing spectacle of shame and derision.

Indeed with great DREAD have we, the children of earth's choicest, looked upon our complexion and the plight of our sojourn. Surely did father Adam question well regarding the time of the reversal of our disfavor. With abject consternation and pitiful angst of heart have we walked through the corridors of time. What is this damning heaviness that persists unabated upon those who bear the blessing of divine melanin enrobement?

Oh, what killing madness doth come with this remnant of that day which began with evening! When shall come the reversal of disfavor? When shall there come an END?

No GLIB prognostication of things to come resulting from the passing of the Ages, it is neither Pisces, nor Aquarius that holds the remedy to our distress. No RUSE of prosperity in this world's wealth or acceptance will turn what Jehovah has wrought. Too mighty an adversary is He to repel or restrain. Oh, mighty, royal, divine appointed African Brothers and Sisters our controversy is (and has always been) with God. Words of flesh and breath will never revoke His pronouncement of chastisement, nor yet circumvent His sentence to dishonor.

His judgements have made us VASSALS of those whom once we taught in ages past. Those who begged audience with great Kemet, and lightly-barefooted tread in awe, with downward bowed heads, through the coasts of Kush and Ta-Neter, have now become our masters. Cruel masters have they become -- like an ungrateful "gaggle of golems[39]" -- the thing, the civilization we generously civilized now smites the countenance that blessed it and reviles the genius that awakened it. How dimly do they recall that before concourse with our congenial generous hospitality they possessed no civilization at all? All advancement of society, technology, and wisdom came by those who now are averse and impotent to measure the length of the Universe etched upon the span of our cubit. No longer are we counted among men... closer to dim-witted Simian primates are we reckoned within this world we have built.

With what OCULAR illumination must we, the Ancient visionaries, possessors of the eye of Djehuti, be enlightened? Upon what Celestial Meridian lies the sidereal orientation of our Acceptable Year of the Lord? What is it that may remove the blindness too bright from over-glutted retinas flooded with coronal blaze?

Too long have we nostalgically gazed, transfixed upon Horus-Osiris-Amen Ra's[40] iconic glare beneath the nascent light of his evanescent rule. And in the fixation of our hearts upon the sand-built Djed[41] did we lose vision and sight of the Eternal Rock. Indeed has the Eye that was Light now become a relic in the Dark.

The reversal of disfavor lies in the hands and hearts of this generation. Yet, it is not without the AIDE of the One Greater than Africa that we shall again know the lifting of our Discommendation[42]. The day arose and fell that began with night and ended in the morning. In the cool of the evening Yahweh's Perfect Light lifted and our shadow emerged. That first darkened equinox from whence came (the) Fall, mighty Atum's silhouette lengthened eastward into the midnight of that dreadful terminal equinox when the Divine Scepter of the Almighty's Stewardship did Spring from our grasp.

With the death of thousands of our firstborn sons did the coasts of the Nile wail from beneath the edge of Abaddon's, Apollyon's[43] blood-parched Sword. No, unlike Damocles[44], we knew no joy, nor "Pollyannaesque[45]" levity, for in one night-morning-day the pearl of eternity was stripped bare of all its nacre and exposed as naught but vile sun-scorched sand. Too too familiar is today's specter of the hundreds, the thousands of our sons lain strewn in the streets of our villages, the floors of our homes, in the arms of our fathers, mothers and upon the wheels and benches where we work, play, and live. They lie there, even as they lay then, cut down, drawn and quartered - not so much by an enemy, as by our appointed Providential Guardian become an avenging angel. Which angel was the Sentinel, the Champion who opposed and slew all aggressors and any impudent enough to question or yet resent Deity's unspoken but melanin blessings upon our race.

Aye, in this generation, the Generation of PROMISE, does our final opportunity, our Kairos[46] of Destiny await its acknowledgement and entrance into. That Promise from long ago which christened the brow of Negus/Nigiste and sowed woolen spiral galaxies upon our brows, crowns, and napes in the place of locks, follicles, and manes. The promise remains - for the gift of God is without repentance - and He has not revoked His Sovereign Will. He awaits the Steward of Yahweh to awaken from his rebellion. He awaits the Steward of Yahweh to return from his folly. He awaits the Steward of Yahweh to cease from the labor of sinfulness and abomination and REST in His Truth.

And what is this Promise that came so long, suspended so long ago? The promise of fulfilling that charge of Stewards of the Revelation of the Face of the Almighty is that long abrogated legacy. Like Sisyphus[47], all of our gargantuan feats and efforts are counted for nothing that has been strained out under such estrangement from Him. Only the highest boulder may plummet to the deepest depths; only the most anointed angel may become the most wicked devil; only the most liberated and free may become the most oppressed and enslaved; only the most enlightened and principal celestial beacons may become inescapable black hole singularities. We fester in warden-less prisons of time, space, and matter. Without Our Lord Jesus Christ, that which is most prominent is doomed to implode in upon itself under the weight of its own self-vaunting. Have we not travailed sufficiently under the burden of disfavor? Have not our Sins found us out?

Has not history and mystery veritably evidenced that it is El Al, and not ET AL, Whose Favor we must curry? Is it not plain to us in this Fifth Millennium past the "Cross" (of the Passover and blood-drenched entrances) and this Fifth Century past the "Crossing" (of the Middle Passage and blood-stenched trenches) - both witness to willing and wailing exoduses from the Land of Golgotha, Calvary, a place of a skull - that without Him we can do nothing?

Through the "Cross" our ill-hosted Hebrew guests departed, by way of the brow. Carried with them did they the Scepter of Stewardship, which after two days [for a day with the Lord is as a thousand years, and a thousand years as a day] they disdained it beneath the Blood-stained cross... at Golgotha, beneath the impaled feet of Shiloh.

From the base of the Land of Golgotha[48] we deported as bruised, chastised, scourged, smitten, contemned, and parleyed malefactors for the Offense. The Offense that came by failing to KEEP that Sacred Trust, first given to Adam and bequeathed to the offending generation... in the days of Noah then Melchizedek and Akhenaten.

Oh how fickle the vagaries of mortal gratitude! As surely as the sun rises there has arisen this generation that treasures not the mercies of Jehovah. Those blessed benefits that were wrought by prayers prayed beneath pails and under shadow of the stars are now presumed the rights bestowed upon those "excluded" by a begrudging Sophistic Constitution[49]. And how could this generation, long since deafened to the "Analects of the Drinking Gourd[50]," truly know the Concert of Oppression's marooned?

It is time we the Generation of Promise, it is time that we rise up, rather, rise together to acknowledge and embrace our Calling to return to Yahweh that we may be healed. It is time that we put from us the Hod of our GRUESOME Burden, cast it aside for the Glory of proclaiming and entraining in His Communion. The answers to this pernicious persistent injustice and implenitude lie not in a political, economic, or social agenda. No, our salvation lies not in any strategy, philosophy, or cultural retreat. They are ALL *The Verdict of Providence* and pronouncement of *Disfavor* upon a people highly favored but highly treasonous against the Almighty.

The Reversal of Disfavor shall come as we, this generation of Promise, turn to the Almighty, to Yahweh, the Lord Jesus Christ and entreat Him, repent and submit - once again - and we shall be healed. For there yet stings and clings to our palate that bitter FICUS CARICA[51], long ago imbibed, ingested, digested, and indigested by Father Adam, itself arsine - poison lading all that we speak. Ere we may speak again the Metu Neter, the words of God, must we be cleansed from the breath of death, which we both breathe and inspire.

Flee must we the DIN of clamoring dead voices, that vie for deity and worship, yet themselves cannot stave off the ravishes of defanged, declawed death. Flee, aye, yes flee I say we must those impressive imperious demagogues who themselves can impale nor crush masochistic devotees beneath their "juggernautic[52]" wheels, lest some feeble frame bear them about by their unstable staves. Whether it be Al-ilah (dubious first among the days of the sand-blasted lunar year); Buddha the young prince fleeing and finding enlightenment in debilitation; or Shiva destroyer of worlds, or Mary Theotokos[53], herself unexalted above the company of the redeemed, and the host of other myriad contenders for *"god for a day."* Unequivocally must we declare and once again proclaim the exclusive right to worship as residing in the Lord Jesus Christ alone - above all others... this my African steward sibling is the one exclusive way to enter into the Reversal of Disfavor.

Since the Prime Meridian[54] was wrenched from its natural geodetic ley, all time, all reckoning and rhythm of Gifted Alkebu-lan has been out of step. Only dimly does the faint GLINT of a past faded glory glimmer in the opaque memories of the unwilling penitents now groveling before gilded dung heaps... covetously grasping for feasts fit for hyena. Since that time (1884), coincident with the Berlin Conference[55], east was turned backward and the day was arbitrarily shortened. The Reckoning of Time, the Prime Meridian passing through the Bennu of Khufu[56] (the Great Pyramid's Center), was reversed in its station and all of Africa was partitioned and parceled among the nations. All men were thrust out of rhythm - and we lost sense of Hymn.

-The beginning of Day was plunged into Night -
-The Holy VALET became courier to BLIGHT -

East having intruded into West, the entrance of the Temple was made to invade the Most Holy Place… it is no wonder we have come to disdain the Sacred and trivialize the Consecrated. When we return and entreat the Lord, after we repent of our diffidence toward Him, then shall the Common Wandering quit the Vagrant Loitering, fumbling in the Oracle - then shall the Hymn and the Consecrated be restored. Shekinah from Ichabod, light for dust, apothecary for necrosis is the Reward of Holiness.

All that we were as Stewards of the Eternal has been distorted. Now may we return to it. We may make our calling SURE in Him by returning to seek His face and one another's embrace. For truly the first responsibility of an African is another African, this is pleasing unto God!

In this shall we make the SEAL of Divine Favor sure. In this alone shall we enter again into His exalted favor. Only in this shall we know again the active, ceaseless enablement of Jehovah upon Africa - now, to discharge that long suspended charge of countenancing His Light in these closing hours of the day ending in the morning. Let us rise up and enter into His Temple of Prayer. Why sit we here and die?

He has said, "Come unto me and I will give you rest…" let us arise unto holiness in Him. Let us fall upon our knees - not to receive again the strokes of the scourge, but the bestowing of healing and restoration by the Hand of Our Father and the Life of Our Lord. This is our CUE. This time of utter despair and dashing of communal good, from both abroad and within, by which we have continually known defeat, is the time of embracing the Restoration of the Stewardship. The way up is down. Christ Jesus is that Way. For He has said,

> *"If my people, which are called by my name,*
> *shall humble themselves and pray, and seek my*
> *face, and turn from their wicked ways; then will*
> *I hear from heaven, and forgive their sin, and*
> *heal their land."*

Only in this, shall ***Restoration of the Stewardship*** orient upon our present horizon, the loosing of ***Ichabod***[57] and the alighting of the ***Shekinah***. Then, and only then may ***proud poured out Alkebu-lan*** retract his "blurred inverted image from behind the liquid illusive looking glass" and remove the aberration of his ***null ka ba,*** and right ***his ankh,*** so long now bent upon ***Set-wardship.*** Is it not now the fullness of the time in which we must reclaim the ***rest of the oration***, so long ago begun by Atum that first pronounced life upon our crown? ***"O bad chi,"*** have you not yet exhausted the sting of your foul biting necrosis that has sought ravenously to devour our souls?

> This is our CUE. In this shall we make
> the SEAL of Divine Favor sure. We
> may make our calling SURE in Him
> by returning to seek His face and one

another's embrace. Only dimly does the faint GLINT of a past faded glory glimmer in the opaque memories of the unwilling penitents now groveling before gilded dung heaps… covetously grasping for feasts fit for hyena. Flee must we the DIN of clamoring dead voices that vie for deity and worship, yet themselves cannot stave off the ravishes of defanged, declawed death.

For there yet stings and clings to our palate that bitter FICUS CARICA, long ago imbibed, ingested, digested, and indigested by Father Adam, itself arsine - poison lading all that we speak. They are ALL *the Verdict of Providence* and pronouncement of *Disfavor* upon a people highly favored and highly treasonous against the Faithful Almighty. It is time that we put from us this Hod of our GRUESOME Burden, cast it aside for the Glory of proclaiming and entraining in His Communion. The Offense that came by failing to KEEP that Sacred Trust, first birthed in Adam and bequeathed to his offending polluted offspring generation… during the circuits of Noah then Melchizedek and Akhenaten. Has not history and mystery veritably evidenced that it is El Al, and not ET AL, Whose Favor we must curry? He awaits the Steward of Yahweh to cease from the labor of sinfulness and abomination to REST in His Truth.

Aye, in this generation, the Generation of PROMISE, does our time of visitation, our Kairos of Destiny await its acknowledgement and entrance into. Yet, it is not without the AIDE of the One Greater than Africa that we may again know the lifting of our Discommendation.

Surely, as Jehovah built symmetry into forward flowing time, and every evil thing mirrors everything good, so surely is it time that the Good thing built in Jehovah's symmetry be mirrored in every evil. Restoration of our Stewardship commands our return to the Mound of Moriah upon which the perfect sacrifice of Jehovah's gift was offered without reservation, hesitation, or resentment. The thing most desired, most craved, and most defining was by Abraham bound, presented, and consigned to the blade that the Giver of the gift may be denied in nothing and pleased in all things.

Has He not consigned the son of promise to the cord of the altar so far removed to a desolated place? Has He not commanded the God-conflicted act in appointing death to the seed of life, slavery to freedom's light, and contempt upon the image of His complexion? Even as the longed for Isaac, in yielded submission and cooperative resignation, lay upon that pyrrhic cord of wood and beheld (as the muster of Abraham's one hundred and thirty-three years hefted the flint of sacrifice high above head to plunge it into his heart) - in muted resolute silence; so humbled Africa, must we resign to this altar, for it is of the Lord. Without hesitation, without argumentation Abraham swiftly and obediently executed the command to, "sacrifice thy son, thine only son... "

In that distended moment of full gathered tension for the downward thoracic thrust, "Stop!" thundered the angel of the LORD, in duet with the ensnared "bleating" Ram caught in the thorn-woven thicket - the Appointed Substitute.

Let us in this distended moment become resolute in submission. Knowing that Yahweh has not appointed us unto death but unto salvation; even as our bounded stay upon this our altar - slavery and ignominy - has been three and one-half days (the cycle of probation), the Ram has appeared, its bleating now disrupts the specter of the plunging blade. Yes, three and one half days... from that blood drenched vernal equinox under the Aegis of Pesach[58] (1486 Before Christ) until this emergent Spring during the time when the lambs are born (Anno Domini 2002) a full 3500 years. For a day with the Lord is as a thousand years, and a thousand years is as a day, three and one half millennia.

What evidence is there for this momentous cycle... what chronometer, or dial of Ahaz[59] reckons such miraculous release? Throughout Torah, Nabiim, and Chetuvim[60] the gematria of Jehovah is fixed in the affairs of men. His symmetry is unimpeachable. It is by such constant regularity that His ways may be known. Was it not the pronouncement of probation upon the rotted reign of Ahab that the drought prevailed three and one half years at the word of Elijah? And again under the mantle of

Elisha famine persisted twice three and one half years; the tribulation shall blanket the earth, probation of both Israel and the Nations - three and one half, three and one half, seven years. The two resurrected witnesses lay dead in the streets of Jerusalem three and one half days and they were raised again… the ministry of Jesus was three and one half years, as was the probation of Adam (after Eve was made) three and one half years.

Is it small wonder that after three and one half millennia Pan Africa, primeval Pangaea, has come upon the reckoning moment? With every cycle of probation comes a test of resolution. Shall we go the way of Judas[61] (who chose to reject the testimony of Resurrection) or exercise the restraint and conviction of Judah[62] (who stayed the hands of his brothers from annihilating their sole means of salvation)?

Restoration of the Stewardship hangs between an "s" and an "h." It must be Juda<u>s</u> the traitor, or Juda<u>h</u> the praiser. In the Hebrew language it is either Sin[63], or He[64]. In the Metu Neter (words of God) it is Set[65], or Hotep[66], the Serpent or Peace.

Come let us gather ourselves unto Him, and unto Peace. After the third day He has said that He will heal us. Only now let us return to Him and entreat Him that we may be healed, restored, and receive the lifting of our Discommendation in this midst of the Week. For now does there await us, draped across the arm of Jehovah washen, cleansed, and consecrated robes. He stands with expectation ready to enrobe us with our long absented Nilotic Vestments[67]. It is the silence of our un-awakened voices that he longs to hear - once again in the Proclamations of blood bought Salvation.

Let us not pluck again the forbidden thing that thrust us to the ground... let it be life (ankh) and not death, let it be health (seneb) and not the sickness of sin, and let it be peace (hotep), and not fear. Rather, let us stretch our long barren palms unto that Aloe that heals and preserves unto life. He awaits us in the Person of the Tree of Life, the Risen Christ who only is our Garment and our Light.

σ

Surely none were greater, nor can any exceed the healing preservation and emollient wrought into the favored that is the SALVE, the ebon ointment of Jehovah, most anciently known as Atum, both the Man and the Man-maker; one the image and fractal reflection, One the Source and Encompassing Whole.

IN returning, in facing into the western dawn - the Holy of Holies, shall we mighty fallen Africa, erstwhile Eden enter into UNION WITH TRUTH.

May we quit the OCCULT and the demiurge of demons and (m)angels[68] reserved for such horrid flaying flames of torment... why, why will we with willing wilting worsening wanton, work willingly withering wile? Quit the occult, Baptism of Lucifer, engorging with Baphomet[69] and impaling of Orisa[70].

Upon the abandonment of the CULT of self-hatred, self-love, self-worship, and murder will emerge again the light borne from that distant eastern sunset... only then will return the absenting of our oppressive onerous shadow. The dissipation of the blood bloodied streets, the erasure of fear in the day, and the embrace of African upon African in truth and harmlessness.

Quitting our cult, will this very hour unveil our eyes... and with OCULAR acuity shall the vision imparted by Yahweh, the unmade Savior, return and we shall see Him as One people - again. Again, as before when He was wont to walk twice daily among favored Kush at the morning and the evening oblation. With opening of the eyes shall we understand that it has always and ever been the Lord Jesus Christ who is Savior and Sire of our being.

That Blood encrusted unalloyed Scepter of Stewardship solemnly leans half-protruding from its blood-soaked, thorn-sequined dune... undisturbed since the company of Israel cast it aside beneath the brow of Golgotha. From where the Cross once impaled, now gapes from the greave-trampled lacerated ground an unclosed but muted wound, whose vulva achingly purses that twice despised Scepter of Stewardship, now glimmering with humming glow beneath our achronycal dawn. With trembling rigor of millennial pain the earth in Golgotha, Continental and Continua Golgotha[71], Africa dare not gasp for unholy reprieve lest this closing quantum of the day of visitation dim into oblivion. Unlike Israel, let us embrace and straightway proceed into this our Time of Visitation.

Let us, with re-opened eyes take up again this our Scepter of Stewardship. And what is this Stewardship? None other than that declaration and embodiment of the Face of the Holy, the Living God… to give living witness of His Eternal Truth in melanin, burnt brass bodies. To be living sanctuaries, holy and true, to be divine vessels both reflective and refractive of His unutterable wisdom and undimmed countenance, this is our stewardship, this is our scepter.

The entrance into union with truth is the harvest of healing of our people. In such entrance no monarchy, no republic, no institution, no liturgy, or spirit on high or low shall have power or potential to again enslave or impede us.

Then shall we see, truly, what Jehovah intimated when he said, "… I will heal Egypt (Africa) when he returns and entreats the LORD…" this is that day.

When veritably did Egypt, Africa, know the Eternal? From the very beginning, before the days of Abraham did we embrace His unseen light. Before the evening and morning of Moses, Aaron, Joshua, and David, holy, consecrated and wise Eden knew and adored the Almighty and He adored us.

It is now time that we, Africa-everywhere, discard our filthy borrowed garments of ignorant self-mockery, and dumb mimicry of caricaturized shadows. And rather embrace the Truth once and for all delivered on the hill and horn of Golgotha… and at Giza. Only in this shall we again be exalted by Yahweh Himself into that regal and reserved Office of ORACLE of God in the earth.

And if this seems so great a calling and charge, consider that its (hapax legomena[72]) constellation will never orient again. For on the outskirts of every ville, burg, and hamlet, above the hills overlooking every city, metropolis, enclave, and clan the Lord stands watching and listening. Watching the motions of our hearts and this conjunction's degrading orbits toward the fading of this brilliance. He is listening for our surrender of our will to His will, as He listens to the last beads of sand fall free from their crowded congregation in the hourglass' hall. He is listening to the heart of prayer and cursing of every African, He has bent down His ear to listen for our resignation unto Him.

And if it seems an unlikely thing that a people so great and divided should be called upon to answer in concert the Imperative of the Almighty, and if it seems that the Lord, Nkulunkulu[73], has required of us a thing impossible; and if it seems that the eternal destiny of so many hangs on the whim of so many, then consider this, that everywhere the chosen ebon inhabit ground and space - He only requires the Gideon's 300 to come over to Him. He has chosen them to turn the tide for the fearful and the reckless who are always rejected from His service.

Who are they? They, the Gideon's 300 are those men and women who will stand, rather prostrate themselves - now - to the Living God in the Presence of the Living Christ to scatter the enemy that would rob us forever of our heritage.

Gideon's 300 are the powerful, but few who dare to live for Him in abandonment of this flimsy temporal façade… they are the obscure 0.9375 per cent of the unenlightened many.

And if there shall fail of the 300 to come urgently forward to enter into Union with Truth, during this our Last Call under the governance of man, then speedily (like the flight of a famished falcon toward its unsuspecting prey) shall all the giftedness of Africa be taken from her forevermore, and given to another, by the hand of Yahweh Himself.

What say you chosen ones of God, shall you remain a prince (ess) uncrowned, a priest (ess) unconsecrated, or a prophet (ess) unanointed? We have but this one remaining moment to fulfill the expectation of Yahweh and make nil the anxiety of Atum.

Let us no longer live under the veil of evil or the vile, but rather cast from us our libel of the Only Holy One and in Him alone believe!

σ

For then shall the Restoration of our Stewardship fully arouse us to Awakening[74] and usher dignified Holy Africa again into UNION WITH HIM WHO IS TRUTH.

Endnotes:

[1] "Atum" as demonstrated in *Echoes of the Old Darkland* by Charles S. Finch III, M.D., page 145, Chapter V, The Nile Valley Sources of the Old Testament, shows that the Hebrew Adam (the equivalent of the Egyptian-Khemetic Atum) is named after him. Adam is the first man made in the image and named after the perfect Divine Man (See 1 Tim. 2:5).

[2] The name (aspect) of God revealed (emphasized) to Moses at Sinai. From the Khemetic Yah-Wah compound. **Wah** is the lunar aspect of God as Thoth (Djehuti, also Jehudi), Khonsu, or Osiris meaning that he is ruler of the night, hence the spirit realm. **Wah** means to increase, thusly God increasing in manifestation as the ruler of the spirit realm or the night. The Israelites "left by night." Ibid. p. 161. Also see page 173 in Appendix II to read quotations from classical writers attesting to the African Origins of the Early Hebrews.

[3] The ancient name describing primeval earth's single giant continent.

[4] The oldest and the most indigenous ancient name of Africa meaning, "Mother of Mankind" or "Garden of Eden" used by the Moors, Nubians, Numidians, Khart-Haddans (Carthaginians), and the Ethiopians see the Original African Heritage Study Bible, KJV General Editor, the Reverend Cain Hope Felder, PhD, page 102.

[5] The Egyptian cognate (root) of the Hebrew Satan; Satan is the compound word of its dual word cognate Set-An meaning, "the second manifestation of Set (the Evil One). It in fact is, since Set, once Lucifer fell from his celestial estate. See Finch, page 165.

[6] Egyptian cognate of the Hebrew Adonai, the substitute term for Yahweh. Where the term "Lord," as distinct from "LORD" is used, it is translated from the Hebrew *Adonai (אדני)* meaning Lord as ruler. The Hebrew word translated LORD is from the Hebrew *Yahweh (יהוה)*, this distinction is most used in the KJV.

[7] Ankh is the Metu Neter glyph and word for life.

[8] Duat is the term referring to the duality of the terrestrial world below and celestial world above. It also referred to the reality that joined the two.

[9] Per-aah is the Kemetic word translated Pharaoh in the Hebrew, meaning the Great or White House (palace of the pharaoh) which symbolized both him and his office.

[10] Maat is the ancient science, philosophy, and theology system of ancient Africa, i.e. truth, justice, and righteousness.

[11] Sakhu is the principle of wisdom.

[12] Negus, Nigiste are variant masculine and feminine forms of the most ancient African name of God, viz. Ngr, Nga - Niger, Niggar, Nigger. See *Original Names of God and Jesus* by Dr. John Johnson.

[13] Apis is the bull representation of the deity Osiris (as it is a metaphor of Jesus, the Servant of Yahweh) as well as the celestial Constellation of Taurus. It is associated with the sacrifice of bullocks and the red heifer. It was just before the constellation or sign of Taurus the Bull that the season of Passover, Pesach occurred.

[14] Ptah is one of the variant names used to describe the creative activity of God. The word means to "spit out." It is used in New Testament Scripture - transferred into the Aramaic - when Jesus spoke to the dumb man and said, "Ephphatha," meaning be opened. Mark 7:34. Ptah through creation opens up the material order.

[15] Based on the corrected chronology of David Davidson detailed in *The Date of the Exodus of Israel*, the entry of Joseph occurred ca. 1711 B.C. during the 18th Dynasty under the 1st or 2nd year of the sole regency of Pharaoh Thutmosis III. He was the stepson of Hatshepsut Queen Pharaoh and wife of the late Thutmosis II. According to Davidson's outstanding synthesis of all ancient secular and Biblical chronologies the Exodus occurred in the year 1486 B.C. This was, according to the Talmud five years after the death of Ramses II, consequently the Pharaoh of the Exodus was Merenptah his 13th son (whose autopsied lungs were filled with salt water - due to drowning). *See Koinonia House Newsletter article on Merenptah.*by Chuck Missler.

[16] Peribsen was the 2nd Dynasty Pharaoh that established Set, i.e. Satan worship in ancient Egypt. See *Who Were the Pharaohs* by Stephen Quirke.

[17] Pishon and Gihon are ancient African (and Amharic) names of the White and Blue Nile Rivers. See *The Original African Heritage Bible.*

[18] The Metu Neter, called hieroglyphics by the Greeks, means the *words of God (the gods).* The Greek emphasis is on the characters themselves, however it was the entire system of sacred, philosophic, and scientific communication so expressed. In Egypt, Kemet, it was the system of communication exclusive to the priests and highly educated. In Ethiopia, i.e. Ta-Neter, it was the common language and script.

[19] Cain, Abel, and Seth were the three special sons of Adam and Eve that bore divine potential, but were ineligible to redeem man. In the history of Ethiopia is recorded that Adam and Eve had 50 to 55 sons and daughters. See *The Real History of Ethiopia.*

[20] Ta-Neter is the ancient indigenous name of primeval Ethiopia

[21] Adami is one of the names given to the offspring of Adam during Ante-diluvian days.

[22] See Ezekiel 28:14, KJV of the Bible.

[23] See Isaiah Chapter 14:12-14.

[24] See Revelation Chapter 4 and 5.

[25] The Sapphire Sea of Glass is the Pavement before the Throne God upon which the worship of God and the judgment of all things, in heaven, occur. See Exodus 24:9-11; Ezekiel 1:16; 10:1; 28:14; Revelation 4:3,6; 15:1,2

[26] See Ezekiel 28:14-19.

[27] A Galactic Year is the duration of one revolution of our solar system's sun about the center of the Milky Way Galaxy, i.e. 200 Million Years.

[28] Cydonia, the name given the Northern Hemisphere of the planet Mars and site of the Face. This artificial monument discovered amidst the 1979 Surveyor photographs reveals an African "simian" face sporting a Nemis crown (worn only be African Pharaohs. Sophisticated imaging technology further revealed the

Face crying - one tear falling from the right eye. The Face is situated 8 to 10 miles from a City of Pyramids.

[29] Twin asteroid moons of Mars.

[30] The menoi were pre-Adamic men that lived before the Flood of Lucifer, see Genesis 1:2; Isaiah 45:18; and Jeremiah 4:23-25.

[31] Leviathan is the most dreadful incarnation of Satan, as described in Job 41. He is the formidably irresistible and unconquerable foe of man. He is fearless and disdainful of all puny mortal weaponry. He is a metaphor for the enemy only God could bring to defeat.

[32] Djehuti, the Kemetic name of the God's divine aspect of wisdom and the source of such; the Greeks called him Thoth and to the Romans he was known as Hermes.

[33] Ta Neter, the Land of God, i.e the Garden of Eden (Aten) - Ethiopia.

[34] Ta Meri is one of the ancient Khemetic names of Egypt.

[35] An Adept was one that had mastered the principles of the 42 Books of Hermes (Djehuti, Thoth). This one was indeed a Sage, viz. a master scientist-priest that knew the secrets of the Universe and Cosmic laws. The so-called magi(cians), actually, wisemen - scientist-mystics, Jambres and Jannes exercised this knowledge by transforming their staffs into not cobras, but crocodiles. The Hebrew word translated *serpent* is *thanniin (תאנין)* is Dragon, the monster of the Nile, hence the crocodile. Please take note that Aaron first transformed his rod into a "crocodile" after which the Adepts did likewise. It is distinct from the serpent in the Garden of Eden, translated from the Hebrew word *nachash (נחש)* from the hissing and deadly bite. See *Wilson's Old Testament Word Studies.* MacDonald Publishing CO. McLean, VA.

The Adepts are called the wise men and sorcerers in the Exodus Chapter 7:9-13. The Hebrew words translated *wise and sorcerer,* respectively are *chacam (חכם) and chashaph (חשף).* The meaning they carry have been corrupted through indirect transmission from language to language. The wise men of ancient Kemet were first of all scientist priests who had completed 40 years of deep study and discipline in the divine science and knowledge of the Universe, Self, and God. They were scientists, philosophers, and priests of divine truths. The term sorcery refers to their knowledge of chemistry and quantum physics. The word chemistry - al kemetu - means the Egyptians. The Greek translates this word sorcery from *pharmekeaia*, the root word for pharmacy and drugs. The word for wise men is *magi*, which is borrow word from the Persian. From Humphrey *Priddeaux's History of the Jews* we learn that the word magi is a Greek contraction of the Persian *mige-gush, meaning the cropped eared.*

In the court of Cyrus, King of Persia - deliverer of Israel, one of the counselors of was found guilty of a misdemeanor punishable by mutilation. His punishment was the cutting off of his ears. Because he was one of the most trusted counselors and wise men of Cyrus all of the counselors from that point in time ca. 6th Century B.C. were called - *Mige - Gush, i.e. the cropped eared.* When Alexander conquered Persia the term passed into the Greek language without the benefit of the history of the term. It was a label of derision and mockery. No such meaning was attached the Adepts of Egypt (See Isha Schwaller de Lubicz's *Her Bak).*

[36] Seshep ankh Atum is the most ancient name of the divine monument built on Giza Plateau, of which the word Sphinx is the Greek corruption. It means the living image of Atum. Atum is none other than Adam of Genesis Chapters 2 - 5, who was created in the image of God. Seshep ankh Atum is the surviving image of the Pre-incarnate Christ and creator of Adam-Atum. See footnote on Atum.

[37] Giza is the site of Seshep ankh Atum and ancient reflection of the Constellation of Orion during the age prior to the global flood of Noah, i.e. Zep Tepi.

[38] See Isaiah Chapter 19:1-25.

[39] Among the various versions of the East European Jewish legend one has it that the golem is man-creature made from mud, sticks, and weeds. Once the true name of God is spoken over it, the golem comes alive. On the first day the golem calls it creator *master,* the second day *friend,* and on the third day *servant or slave.* It is from this concept that the golem of Lord of the Rings is taken.

[40] This string of divine names depicts the oneness of the Son of God (Horus) with God the Father in the revelation of the Godhead in the Cosmos and Society.

[41] Also called the spine of Osiris, it represents eternal stability and principle upon which the Cosmos is built.

[42] Discommendation is the stripping of Africa's divine honor and favor in the earth. The time arrived when Africa, rather Alkebulan was no longer revered by its offspring civilizations or itself.

[43] See Revelation Chapter 9:11; Abaddon and Apollyon are names of the Destroyer angel, employed by God to wreak judgment upon the disobedient and rebellious. Although he is the king of the bottomless pit, not Satan, he is called forth on dread summons from God to revel in his nature - to destroy. Refer to Hebrews 12:9; on an occasion where an evil spirit was summoned by God to foment deception and destruction see 2 Chronicles 18:18-22.

[44] Damocles was a Greek nobleman who sat the banquet table of King Dionysius of Syracruse, the richest city of 5th Century B.C. Sicily. Having glibly remarked to his friend the king that he would give anything to trade places for an evening to enjoy his profound bliss and wealth, Dionysius obliged him. At the banquet table Damocles suddenly looked up to discover a very sharp sword dangling above his head - suspended by a single horse's hair. Whereupon his foolish mirth instantly paled into despair and fear, the king said to him, *" . . . like the sword suspended above your head this evening, I live with the constant threat of death and treachery every moment."* Damocles learned that the rich and powerful live with impending dangers - and fears. He never again wished to trade places with the king. See *James Baldwin's Retelling of the Sword of Damocles.*

[45] Pollyanna is the metaphor of "naïve optimism" in the face grave circumstances, a refusal to acknowledge very real and present dangers.

[46] This word means a "window of opportunity" with the underlying sense of a decisive but very short time within which to realize a great advantage or to accomplish a "once in a lifetime aspiration."

[47] Sisyphus was a mythological character condemned by the gods to an eternity of futility by rolling a huge boulder up a high mound only to have it roll to the bottom again. His torment was in repeating this gargantuan feat continually - never to receive satisfaction from his efforts.

[48] The name Golgotha means, *a place of a skull,* and Africa is the only continent that is shaped like a skull. The hill outside Jerusalem where Jesus was crucified is Golgotha, Calvary in the Latin, as well as the land bridge extension of Northeast Africa.

[49] The Sophistic Constitution refers to Article I, section 2,3 defining *Negroes and Native Americans* as 3/5 of a person for voting purposes, and therefore not a person. There has since been a modification removing the clause from the body of the Constitution. The inclusion of the Negro Act, authorizing slavery and legalizing the oppression of Africans, at once relegated the founders of civilization forever to servitude. Furthermore, for those Africans enlightened as to their true heritage, i.e. Moors, they were exempt from the Negro Act under the Moorish Clause of the Constitution ca. 1788. (See Website "Moorish Paradigm"). The term Moor was used as a national ethnic description of Africans as early as 400 B.C., long before the inception of Islam. The force of the Moorish Clause in the U.S. Constitution is that it tacitly acknowledges that the founders of North America, Central, and South were African Moors ca. AD 400. At the time it was called *Amexem!* The name America means, *the land of the black Moors,* in Italian.

[50] During the North American slavery of Africans many slaves escaped winding their way north to safety via the Underground Railroad. The "Drinking Gourd" (Constellation of Ursa Major, i.e. the Big Dipper and North Star) was their guide to freedom. Encoded in the song, *"Follow the Drinking Gourd"* fleeing slaves were given instructions for escape.

[51] Ficus Carica is the fig tree and tree of the fruit of the knowledge of good and of evil. See Genesis 3:6.7.

[52] The word juggernaut is derived from the Hindu *JagganAth.* It is Sanskrit for *"lord of the world"* which was a deity worshiped in Puri, a town in the Indian State of Orissa. Each year an idol representing the god is taken from its temple and dragged on a

huge wooden cart to a nearby house by hundreds of pilgrims. Frenzied pilgrims would throw themselves beneath the massive wheels of the cart (parade float) which crushed them to death. From this practice the word juggernaut was derived meaning an invincible force. Properly, the god's name was *Jaggan,* and those pilgrims were the *JagganAths* who worshipped him in that sacrificial fashion. See *South Asian Journalists Association* site www.saga.org.

[53] The Emperor's sister, Pulcheria, introduced this term, Theotokos, into the Ecumenical Council of 381. Consequently, Mary was elevated to the station of worship and by decree of the Church declared to be the *"Bringer forth of God."* This is in direct opposition to Scriptural teaching, God has no beginning (See John 8:58). She was rather the *Christotokos, the bringer forth of Christ.*

[54] The Prime Meridian is the natural Longitude of Zero Degrees, it is the beginning of day and the first moment of time as reckoned geographically on earth. As one travels east the day or time proceeds. Going backwards, i.e west one travels towards the previous day of global time.

[55] Berlin Conference was the 19th Century European Conclave in which Africa was partitioned into regional colonial possessions of England, Germany, France, Portugal, etc. for economic benefit and political hegemony. Principally organized by Chancellor Otto von Bismarck of Germany the Conference was in session from November 15, 1884 to February 26, 1885 and attended by 14 European Nations (including the United States of America). What resulted was the artificial political division of Africa into 50 European dominated countries - the exceptions being Ethiopia and Liberia.

[56] The apex of the Great Pyramid of Khufu is the natural Prime Meridian of earth, as well as the center of the geographical global land mass. Its assignment to Greenwich, England was an artificial and arbitrary relocation of the natural day and reckoning of time. Presently, time under GMT, i.e. Greenwich Mean Time (UT) is reckoned more than two hours "behind." Morning truly was pushed into night by 31^0.

[57] The word *Ichabod* means, "glory has departed." See 1 Samuel 4:12-22.

[58] Aegis of Pesach is the Passover, the protection Israel received at the Exodus.

[59] The sundial used by Hezekiah to reckon time. Its shadow (or beam of light) was turned backward by 10 degrees; time was reversed, as a sign that God had given him 15 additional years of life. See Isaiah 38:4-8.

[60] The Hebrew Bible, the Tanach, is divided into three sections - the Torah (Law), Nabiim (Prophets) and the Chetuvim (the Writings).

[61] It is traditionally taught that Judas "hanged" himself on the morning of the Crucifixion. Close examination of the Scriptures, e.g. 1 Corinthians 15:1-5; Matthew 10, reveals that Jesus appeared to the twelve after His resurrection which also included Judas. Rather than believe the Deity of Christ and repent - he hanged (disemboweled) himself, see Acts 1:18; 2 Samuel 31:4, **after** the resurrection. At the Ascension of Jesus outside Jerusalem the angel gave the farewell unto the men of *Galilee.* Judas was the only apostle from Judea, to which no reference is made.

[62] See Genesis 37:23-27.

[63] Sin, the Hebrew letter "s".

[64] He (pronounced Hey) is the Hebrew letter "h".

[65] Set is the Egyptian Satan.

[66] Hotep is peace.

[67] Priestly garments of ancient Nubia and Egypt.

[68] These are the nephiliim and offspring of angels and daughters of men, children of Anak - giants.

[69] One of the names of Satan as worshipped, venerated in the lodge of Freemasonry.

[70] Occultic religion, OrishaIfa whose messenger is Legba, a variant form of Set, Satan.

[71] Continental and Continua Golgotha are the land (Africa) and its people (Pan-Africans) spread throughout the world.

[72] In the Greek language this phrase means that a word, term, or item is mentioned only once. Anything that is hapax legomena is a single occurrence within the context it appears.

[73] Nkulunkulu is the name given to God by the Zulus, meaning *"The Great Great God."* See pages 14, 22 of *African Religions:A Symposium edited by Newell Booth.*

[74] Return and entrance into reconciliation and communion with the Lord Jesus Christ and the Holy Father, through the agency of the Holy Spirit. See Isaiah 19:19-22; Acts 4:11, 12; 26:18.

About the Author:

Dr. Jones is an author, composer, director, producer of a number of published plays, a full length musical drama (Gospel Opera), songs and compositions, poems, inspirational prose narratives and elegies. Among his prolific creations he has written several books - Anagrams of Dialectic Antithesis, The Christmas That Began in Africa, Instructions to Godly Men, and Journal of Effectual Prayer, etc. He has as well produced a series of Biblical Studies and Commentaries, several series of published academic curricula and study texts, and video seminar series.

He is a keynote speaker, lecturer, facilitator, business/ education consultant, and motivational presenter to international, national, and local audiences ranging from foreign and domestic government officials to Community/Church audiences.

He holds Ph.D., MBA, and BLS degrees in Higher Education/Learning Styles, Marketing, and Organization Administration, respectively. Dr. Jones is the Executive Director and President of Wisdom Institute Education District and Wisdom Institute University, respectively. He is a graduate and undergraduate professor at National Louis University and St. Louis Community College.